STAR SIGHT GATHERING

Published by Dreaming Deer Press
Marietta, GA, USA 30067

ISBN-13: 978-0692638651

ISBN-10: 0692638652

Cover design by artist Emily Lupita, 2016.

Printed in the United States of America

For poetry books, CDs & DVDs
by Joseph S. Plum, please visit:

www.JoePlum.com

Star Sight Gathering

Joseph S. Plum

Preface

The poems written in this book were transcribed from the original oral poetry that was crafted in the bardic tradition of dreaming and living a lifetime in connection with nature. With spoken word comes a variety of exchanges. Often the word, "I" formats an expression. This "I" may be likened to the rush of air passing through a wooden flute during a skilled performance; at once proclaiming existence of instrument, sound, and atmosphere channeled.

The hope is that by writing down the poems and collecting them into books, they may travel widely and be shared with the world. If you have a chance, please say these poems aloud. In this way, the beauty and power of traditional bardic poetry will live on through your voice.

Artist's Statement

unsettled destiny
shall walk about,
a lantern of dream light
cradled in each hand.

-Joseph Samuel Plum, 2016

Contents

for the giants

who sleep among us,

sometimes visiting

in their dreams

no matter

how many handfuls

are thrown

someday

every skipping stone

must settle

alone

out lined

there could have been
poetry this morning,
a thoughtful emergence
of sensitive words.
yes, there could have been
poetry this morning,
a window to bridge
between two worlds.
there might
be poetry by noontime,
standing full-face
beneath the ark of the sun.
there might be
poetry in my mind
a simple way
to leave my doing undone.
there should be poetry
by evening,
watching as darkness

falls from the sky.
yes, there should be poetry
mixed with dreaming,
moments of liquid emptiness
gliding from the heart
to awaken the eye.
   there will be
poetry by midnight,
sleeping in the stillness
of unmeasured time.
yes, there is always
poetry at midnight,
a mosaic
of graceful intensity,
rich in rhythm and rhyme,
a tapestry
of starlit blackness
back stitched
with silence
of the resourceful kind.
   there must be poetry
in my living,
a pathway of memory

skillfully outlined,

enduring words

of deep understanding

fleshed out in feelings

sweet and sublime,

a pulsating language

of vertical wisdom

unfolding

with the greatest treasure

a seeker can find:

an ancient method

of preserving in essence

a message

that reason never defines,

the secret,

a mystery

of unbounded being

content now

for the moment

to remain

partially hidden

by these quiet spaces

between the lines.

yes,

there could have been

poetry this morning…

starlord

must we hasten
old age with sorrow
will it not come
of its own tomorrow
turning to fruit
our most youthful flower
releasing to seed
our most sovereign power
dissolving us again
like water into mist
as eternity's gateway veil
relentlessly lifts
to reveal heaven's fields
sown with an earthly bliss
that waits to be harvested
by a heart that captures
what these eyes will always miss

please awake my heart
from beneath the hill
in the east

sleeping still

may deepening visions

come one by one

each morning

with the rising sun

gather around me

starlord of infinite sight

wash away

the shadows of the night

bathe me

in your glowing light

that i might see

the beauty

of this day

life has given me.

desert years

a painter of deserts
labored for years
laying grain upon grain
and tear upon tear
before the sun rose
and after the moon fell
he struggled not to struggle
or drop into hell
finally the artist had finished
and he knew he'd done well
for around him stretched
the mountains of sand
all that had sprung
from the tips of his hand
all that he'd lost
and all that he'd found
reached up to meet him
and it pulled him down
as the ground rushed
to greet him
with a sigh

and a thud

he tore his heart

and he lost his blood

which flowed across

the endless sand

to fill the portrait

that the painter

called man

    now the painter's been gone

for many a year

though his paints and his brushes

both are still here

    begin in the middle

and end at the start

trust in your luck

and follow your heart

when you do this with ease

you've done your part

to give to yourself

what can't be taught

the talent to turn

everyday life

into a work of art.

salt water call

flowing out
across rough waters
beneath a cloud formed
from the tears
of the mist dawn mother
down to this river
come the whirlwind whispers
beating to a froth
waves of voices inside of me
saying green are the pastures
that feed the fishes of the sea
black is the drink
of tomorrow's wishes
clear to the bottom
of yesterday's riches
where silver is the fog
about to fall
between rains in the delta
where the water tastes
of upstream, midstream, and all
except for that moment

when the currents lie still
and the wind blows backward
with the saltwater call

   "child" it whispers
"child stand tall"
all children are born knowing
which way to crawl
yet one day walking
starts with a stumble
then running with a fall.
   child come quickly
the clouds await
welcome to the ocean
every young raindrop's fate.

star sight

    hollow
rings the echo
around these sovereign hills
at night
    bright the eyes
of the wandering children
grown older
rimmed with liquid firelight
    broken
is a hoop of willow
bent beyond bounds
by destiny's awesome might
when spoken is the will
of the shining blue icon
each word sparkling
with refracted star sight
    swift are the thoughts
which fly like arrows
into the rising belly of night
cutting away
at this side of darkness

with eyes that flash
like the edge of a knife
    great is the wind
as it sweeps down the narrows
clearing out clutter
from a compromised life
creating an air
charged with potential
one just right
for breathless flight
    where are the dreams
which gather like rainbows?
sweet children
of ambition's furious might
are they high above us?
weaving an anthem of color
a banner
whose promise spans
the bulk of our lives
    there is a way
which leads into seeing
beyond the memories
that screen out original sight

it is here among us

hidden in the depths of believing

we truly know the difference

between wrong and right

    for soft are the steps

of the life force ascending

into the twilight vapors

of a primordial sky

where broken by increments

into constricted potential

long ago love

in the ancient ways

stopped flowing

and gave

the rest of eternity

time

to pass us on by

     now we are like islands

surrounded by oceans

now we are like clouds

climbing out of the sea

now we are like starlight

waiting for darkness

holding

to a power in our hearts

that can set this world free

    look to the landscape

for a view in the morning

gaze into the eyes

of this earth at our feet

carry the moment

like a child who is hungry

alive with feeling

that tomorrow might be

    near is the day

which moves into feeling

a vertical departure

from the lateral fields

spiraling ascension

into stunning retention

as the oscillating aspects of duality

begin to congeal

    go with the voices

returning to wholeness

join with the warriors

who no longer compete

trust in the future

with a heart full of freedom

longing to sustain

but never repeat

    here is the way

that leaps into being

there is the platform

at the base of our feet

here is today

in the service of tomorrow

what more could we need

to be complete?

dream story (in unison)

Here is a poem titled, "in unison." This poem is right straight out of dreaming. It was late December in Iowa. I had been out walking in the fading light. It was snowing and I was quite a ways back in the timber on a high ridge. I remember that I saw 28 deer, all of them walking quietly together as snow and darkness fell. This is a lot of deer. After they had disappeared into the night, I went back home and fell asleep. Immediately I dreamt that I was back among the deer, who were still walking that hilltop in the snow and the dark.

The deer were not afraid of me. They were in a formation of sorts, all travelling north. Each one, every deer, had a personality. I moved in and out between them, watching and listening. Eventually they lost me. I found myself down in a ditch looking into a dark hole at the base of an embankment. Pushing aside a few tree roots, I crawled inside what seemed to be a small cave. To my surprise I could hear water running. The cave turned out to be a tunnel. Following the passage towards a distant light, I suddenly stepped out into what was, really, a different world.

A world of soft yellow and brown light. There was a path, a stone path, which led off over the horizon. At some distance, to the left side of the path, stood a small, rounded hut with an open doorway. I could see some small part of what was inside. There was a flickering light that illuminated an elderly woman seated on a straight-backed wooden chair. Beside her stood an old man. His hand was on her shoulder, with his other hand he motioned for me to enter. And I went into the hut. At the far end there was a fire burning in a stone hearth. A semi-circle of children sat facing the old ones. They were waiting for me.

The man said to me, "You've come. Open your mouth."

And I said, "Given the breath and the…"

He shook his head, said, "No."

And I said, "No one knows the steps…"

He said, "No."

And I said, "These are the days of passage under the sign of the promise given."

Again he shook his head. "No."

And then I said, "Silver haired, the lion lays down with the sheep…"

And he said, "Yes."

Then I said the complete verse. And when I woke up, I knew that poem. And I'd never heard it before! It's called, "in unison."

Notes:
1. The children are the great-grandchildren of the sleeper in time who awake with the advent of insight.
2. The elderly man is my direct ancestor. The woman is my ancestral mother. Always a warm, strong bond.
3. This poem/dream came about over twenty years ago. Still it is more than a memory; it is an open doorway.

in unison

silver haired the lion
lays down with the sheep
not being tired or hungry
with no desire to eat
when he opens his mouth
it's simply to teach
but the lambs hear only a roar
and quickly retreat
to the safety of a flock
where every creature will agree
that to baa
is the one proper way to preach
to baa or to roar
neither one is complete
where every man is half lion
and two-thirds sheep
and the only thoughtful sound
in unison that both can reach
comes when we dream we awake
while still asleep
from the voice of a memory

who stands on its own two feet

by taking from every lesson

the impulse to receive

and giving in return a feeling

in which reason can believe

so that ourselves and our future

can be forever freed

from the struggle of a heart

afraid to bleed

for fear of the lion

who has come

to lay down

with the sheep.

twilight reign

on this earth
our feet are resting
in the distance
our eyes have settled
across the horizon
our thoughts are now reclining
oh, how the crickets
and little frogs were singing
in those first days
of an early autumn.
winter's silence
came soon upon them
they could feel
the cold night returning
beneath the leaves
they stayed on their journeys
while here on this earth
their feet were resting.
who will listen
for you at sunset
and carry your shadow

towards the dawn

no one knows

the steps you have taken

or the way i will

greet the sun

when beneath the clouds

on a mountain of dreams

our feet are resting

as the twilight reign begins

while in the fields below

the homeless are whispering

to each other in the wind

they say that the green

is all too quickly leaving

that their time in this world

has reached an end

then turning to me

with gentle faces

they ask

will you not come with us

into the heartland

of all places

and watch

as our children drop

from beneath our skin

do you not know

the voice of remembering

that leads across

a threshold

into the home

of the wolf

who is a friend

you do not know

that here on this earth

our feet are resting

while far away

into the future

our spirits have been

to teach ourselves

the songs

the little ones are singing

that we might call them

back from the silence again

when on the edge of extinction

we travel together

to clear out the pathways

for the passing
of a few true men.

    all but forgotten
this forever dwelling
this horseless rider
whose heart is galloping
towards the ragged throats
of winter
never begotten
by skillful arguing
this childlike offering
who insists on telling
of prenatal ancient beginnings
underlying
every physical sensation
undying
in the face of seasonal change
time out of mind
we will again become blessed
as we become "us"
once ignited by design
the light in the eyes

of the unnamed one

flames up.

    born of the blood

of burning desire

on the tip of my tongue

is the taste of fire

as these words each turn

to ashes then dust

birth follows death

as always it must

spoken in the hopes

of renewing a vow

while drawing shade

out of shadow

a language of light

was released somehow

it was a question of harmony

focused on a movement within

and although

the answer was balance

the solution

is brought about

by listening

to the gospels of the wind.

    alone

each of us has been left to find

a thread that unravels

the fabric of space and time

not to be afraid

is very hard to do

when heaven and earth

in all their might

have made only one of you

as the momentum of generations

begins to unwind

the spirit who moves

steps forward to redefine

the principle commitment

that connects body to mind

and then shadows

from the moon and the sun

shall overlap

while the multitudes from creation

speak up

on their own behalf.

    after the touch

of those who are

much more than us

all that remains

to be expressed

is that in the old gods

the young ones must trust.

    no dream nor fantasy

not unspoken desire

can bring to the forefront

the virtues of fire

like sleeping in the cold

in concert

with being hungry and tired

no fable or metaphor

nor mythological past

can sanctify ritual into a feeling

that the heart can grasp

unless first rooted in heavens

and then in blood held fast

for truth entertains no notion

that will not last.

royal companion

in winter
fire is a royal companion
born out of kinship from old
where lifetime after lifetime,
wrapped in a robe of darkness,
a dreamer's destiny
takes years to unfold
until up from the lowest seat
of high position,
clear to the noble head
of a living throne,
there flames a procession
of bright intuition
burning with compassion,
elements
from the wandering unknown.
in the north a star has risen
beyond the sight of mortal men
while in the space and time that's given,
from inside,
a storm cloud approaching

signals the beginning

of the middle of the end.

    so many children like to play with fire

though few have ever learned

how to grasp a life of passionate desire

without first getting their fingers burned.

who can sense an open doorway

when in blindness hands are busy passing on?

better still to be still

and enter in the timeless byways

where the warmth within leads

into a greater light beyond.

    across the battle ramparts,

the shining ones came from afar

to rest upon the wind-stilled waves,

disguised as the shimmering of a star.

if you seek to join

with the vanishing rays

of a living sun at twilight

as darkness begins again

to retake the sky,

travel now

beyond the boundaries

long ago established

by too much use of either eye.

   while passing over the portals

each life spans the abyss,

opening and closing with memories

our bodies begin to believe

in a tune filled with sorrow and bliss.

for laid upon our bones is a rhythm

of muscle and fiber entwined in slumber,

a dreamsong

whose singers sleep down under

this blanket of flesh

and that covering of stars

without number

until in the fullness of time,

awakened by pure light

washing the mind,

the guardian of total harmony

begins to appear,

first by sucking silence

out of the inner ear,

then by creating chaos

for anyone near.

if you begin to believe
these words that you hear,
know now
the edge of this world
can be very near,
and dragons in the dark
and deserts in the air
follow each other,
one by one,
until you thirst for breath
and burn from fear,
until quite suddenly,
with notice to none,
you just simply disappear.

and so it is
that the song remains
long after the singer is gone.
and so it is
the dream's unchanged
even though the dreamer awakes
to move on.

and so it is

that the fire leaps

from the flame

to claim the hearts

of those who would do wrong.

and so it is

that when the new day comes

there are so few of us left

to greet the dawn.

and so it is

that fire is a royal companion

born out of kinship from old.

solstice

    i have sat

in the presence of the queen

and made my request

to her attentive keepers

i have given gifts

of honeyed water

and restful sleep

in the valley of the north wind seekers

i was made to be a pole

in the medicine lodge

on the day

of the old god's returning

where i knelt and watched

as the faithful bowed down

at the end of their thirst for learning

    i travel now

on the shadow path

that rattles out

from the throat of winter

following a fire in the east

as it gives way

to the humble promise

of a troubled beginner

who lives

to play a part

in the roundness of all things

curving back into an empty center

which neither gives nor asks

for what

i just can't remember.

   until i have

taken up in these hands

from beneath

the dark flowing water

the chalice of my heart

cradled in the arms

of the earth goddess's daughter

to gather in sweetness

my mother's milk

at the breast

of a cold stony boulder

where bathed

in the gray light

of this false dawn

her children stay young

while the world

grows ever older.

   i have reached

the northern limits

of every sea of thought

where each surface spray

freezes into feeling

then falls to shore

in the shape of dreams

filled with hidden meaning

that transform themselves

whenever i speak

into icy graves

opening at my feet

each a readied resting place

for the dying embers

of a smoldering faith

whose final flame was smothered

by my own disbelieving

   for yes,

i have ridden with the king

in his search

for a true tomorrow

and i still stand

outside that ring

of those who would gain

through other's misfortunes and sorrow

though my vision has suffered plainly

at the hands of time

still in my heart

i know what comes to mind

when again i see

that certain sign

etched

into someone else's eyes

most completely

for yes, i have sat

in the presence of the Queen

and her hand

touched my face

so sweetly.

oracle

just as these words
are like smoke
so the same
my heart is a fire
it's a blood
of forest and wind
that i require
or else as ash
to this earth
i'll soon retire
my crackling flame burnt
of its own desire
without wood and air
i have no choice
no mouth to give
my breath this voice
no sounds to ring
and echo in the mind
bringing forth from silence
many thoughts divine

    in the wildness

where wisdom grows

there is a tree

whose fruit

no one knows

on a branch

that separates

day from night

there sleeps there

in solitude

a many splendid delight

among the stones

who have grown

cold and dark

there awaits there

a hidden silver spark

a tongue of light

not yet to be

a birthless blaze

of unmatched poetry.

    down a tunnel

of spirit wings

through a soundfall

of translucent dreams

above and beyond

all earthly things

heaven loves

a wind that sings.

    turn

and greet the sky

where it meets the earth

pour out your feelings

for all their worth

then stay

to touch the hills

as they grow dark

to cry as though

you've lost you heart

blood, hair, flesh, and bone

together

these become as nothing

when the very next wind that blows

comes to claim your breath

for its very own.

karmic pool

there is nothing
spirit would not give
to those who
are want to steal
except perhaps
warm laughter
on smooth sunshine
or moonlight
bent across the window sill

the parents
of our father's generation
took their turn
upon the wheel
building the foundations
of a fortress of wrong and right
that crumbles now
beneath the weight
of all that's real

when i was young
i stayed inside
their house of silence

guarding what i feel

like all children

born alone

with no way to cry

i was given wounds

that can never heal

    to caress the shore

the swimmer rested

wave in hand

to ride your emotions

to the source

in the darkness

the ocean's voice demands

all life is connected

cries the water

running in

and out the sand

except for those

who are earth bound

and rooted

by a marriage of honor

to the blood

of the clan

and for them

there can be no peace

in their hearts

no way to understand

how to place their feet

upon a bridge of light

and thereby cross over

into the promise land

where no one

ever needs to focus

on the equality of being a man

for all those who go there

arrive without leaving

and take with them

no position

on which to make a stand.

taken to raise

i returned
from the hills of night
to light a fire
in the rain
while all around
unseen phantoms watched
with delight
as the splinters glowed
then broke unbounded
into flame
to call the wind
now at my back
from more than miles away
i edged towards
the sizzling ash
and completely went astray
fire eyes
of a spirits face
gazing outward know
every hidden hollowed place
where rising voices grow

crackling embers

demand a sacrifice

crying out

for a little something

from us all

yet who's to say

what's really at stake

when the dream milkers

come to call

    since that time

i've left my home

and the wind

has taken me to raise

cold and hunger

know me as their own

and share with me

the benefit of their days

    now when the dream milkers

come at night

to feed on those emotions of old

they find me quiet

by the firelight

doing exactly

as i am told

    simply

by the tilt of my head

while i pat

this earth at my side

i give to them

their only dread,

daggers from my eyes,

cut and bleeding

they stumble away

surprising each other

with their new-found cries

which are the first

and only truthful part

of what's been a lifetime

full of lies

    for far too long

they have roamed at will

be satisfying their thirst

with our tears

in stirring up hatred all around

they grow strong

for as long as we run

from our fears

but now i'm the one

who follows them

to bring an end

to their count of years

an end that waits

down this trail of twisted words

that are verbal swords

made up of broken mirrors.

nightwatch

curve of yellow
rimmed with darkness
blue horizon set below
we are the children
of no tomorrows
and we've come to claim
your temples as our home
we bring with us
a pledge of honor
and the valley spirit
from which we've grown
for we are born perpetual
out of joy and sorrow
on the winds
where seeds are sown
in us
high and deep
can come together
bringing into being
each other on their own
like day and night

we must travel in tandem

to and from a time unknown

just beyond your range of vision

one hundred warriors

are waking in a dream

gathering strength

they raise their weapons

by centering

while side stepping

into the mainflow

of your conscious stream

    in our native

mountainous nether regions

as the night watch returns to dawn

campfires of five thousand generations

are being extinguished

replaced by the presence of the sun

at the end of every tunnel vision

deepening shadows are swallowed

one by one

while from the mouth

of those who are believing

each breath issues forth

a wondrous stream of song.

    awake now from within

the sleeping giant

whose throat has long been

a cave to medicine men

gather the harvest of healing power

that's been kept there waiting

clinched in the crystal teeth of the wind

this earth is a beauty

alive with feeling

enthroned without beginning

in a time which has no end

where in a dreamscape barren

and windswept of virtue

alone we must wander

until love takes us

into an awakening

from which our own death

becomes a friend.

the language of birds

there is a secret
to always keep
until there is no one
to keep it from
there is a message
never spoken
until long after
i've lost this tongue
know now
another voice somewhere
will rise up
beneath the setting sun
and give this earth
its closing prayer
in a language
and a scripture
from a time
that's yet to come
grant to me
the free born air
filled with a wind

that will rattle, thunder, and drum

to draw close

those who can truly share

even though

they be deaf

blind and dumb

spirits

need not ears to hear

nor eyes

to see their way clear

to enter our hearts

and make a home there

with room enough to care

for this dream that awakens

through both dark and light

that they and theirs

might sleep to be here

among the margins of any body

with no reason to alarm

or treasures

to guard out of fear

    yes, there is a secret

to forever keep

there is no telling

what is found

emerging out of chaos

and confusion

backwards and upside down

yes i know a secret

learned long ago

as the shorebirds

who were poets

flew away

while calling back to me

over their shoulder wings

with a cry

which seemed to say

    "tomorrow

when we meet again

as promised

in the service

of the coming day

bring with you

the thunder at twilight

to silence

all the spirits

singing on the way

then together

we shall gather

their shadows around us

even as the quiet

begins to fade

that with blood

and dust

and feathered air

a platform for leaping

can be made

for it is only

with the language of birds

the shadows of spirits

and an open heart

that the foundations

of a future age

will be laid

as it is the mixing

of these essential elements

with one other lost ingredient

that this world of ours

shall

from the human race

be saved."

solitary deliverance (the bow song)

the string was there
cutting the darkness
of a dream unbroken
when first that word
of this quest was spoken
releasing with power
the bowsong
whose strength in me
remains as a token
of the archer's arm
long after
his hand has opened
many of my words
are pointed at nothing
they target that emptiness
from which all things grow
like arrows that have been
too long in the quiver
their meanings depend
on what you already know
i will never be

a circle joiner

for i am a flatlander

straight and true

destined by my will

and the laws of nature

to carry the hunt forward

as i pass from view

    that one day

i must come to rest

on the ground is certain

soon after this flight

of feeling is through

even then

the quaking song of the bowstring

will from the inner earth rise up

and tell me what to do

    for yes there is a word

which lies behind every arrow

who has traveled the wind

on behalf of the bow

like a whisper riding

a wave revealing

the image can not help
but to grow and grow
until breaking the barrier
of a sound unspoken
that word comes screaming
down the string again
charging every fiber
in my being with leaving
by filling out my function
with the force of the flow
until the disappearing art
of inheriting motion
is all i have left
with which to show
that the archer's will
is once more intent on bending
as the voice of my instincts
end their sending
by saying soft and low

    "to swallow your loneliness
is the heart of an arrow
be on your way
now quickly, go."

quadrants

i do not grow shallow

as i fall silent

while riding from the rim

to the hub

of the wheel of fate

for i am the spokesman

who has dissected the circle

by cutting a cross

into the middle

in order to reinstate

outward momentum

draped

over an inner movement

which stirs up

the still point

while working to recirculate

all that's before me

into something

forever behind me

as that moment

comes quickly

where the hour seems late

    no i do not grow shallow

as i fall silent

though it might be easy

to make a mistake

and think me

blind, broken and feeble

when in truth

i'm simply stopping

to contemplate

the ways of returning

to an unspoken center

where gravity

will balance out

my spinning weight

by overturning

this feeling of falling

while uncovering

a rolling productive gait

which travels this earth

in search of remembering

the beginnings of building

that wheel of fate

where i first fell shallow

as i grew silent

while moving from the hub

to the rim

of this ancient spiral

we all create.

    if i seem shallow

because i am silent

know

that i've learned

how to watch and wait

as that wheel of fortune

dips down deep inside me

and gathers up again

its once and future

bending shape

that everyday

cuts a track straight

into the heartland of tomorrow

by agreement with the contours

of time and space

until just one single thought

emptied of ambition and desire

counters with a revolution

centered

on a pivot of momentary grace

than all shall be silent

and none will be shallow

as the echo

of these words

tumble into place

and the hum

of that still spinning axle

vanishes

into mid-air

with barely a trace

    for yes

i am the spokesman

who knows

the quadrants

and can draw out the appearance

needed to imitate

nature's prowess

for living in riddles

which speak directly

to the unformed forces

we must one day

turn and face

    that is to say

the wisdom of the ancients

is based on quadrants

then sealed in poetry

composed from nothingness

at a rapid rate

so that no one personality

can adversely reflect reality

when all of everything

is equally made.

    no

i do not grow shallow

even though

i will now fall silent

riding again the rim

of this wheel of fate.

old path

too many roads

when the old path is waiting

no need for mentality

while the heart is debating

the way of remembrance

versus everyday living

as the beauty of this moment

comes wrapped in lifetimes

of eternity forgiving

the changelings of night

for the darkness they're carrying

and the children of light

for the burden of shadows they're sharing

with those who would rather

be reaching beyond

the crosses they're bearing

to uphold the sky

while we drink in the earth

to go out in feeling

until we come back in birth

to sing with brightness

of the ancient ways

to bring in

with lightness

the dawn

of all our future days

    yes, there are too many roads

when the old path is calling

too many roads

once the pale sky starts falling.

through the sky

many wild geese

rise and fall

while within

the path

of their hearts

there is no movement.

About the Author

Joseph Samuel Plum is a direct descendant of Welsh bards and Native American spirit. He lives in South Central Iowa within a group of trees where he composes and presents bardic poetry of original nature. He has been doing this for fifty years. This is his fourth book.

Books by Joseph S. Plum

RELICS

CONCENTRIC DEVOTION

LANDMASS AND OTHER POEMS

STAR SIGHT GATHERING

WHERE RISING VOICES GROW

HUMAN LANDSCAPE

NOBLE REMNANTS

BOOK OF SHADOWS

OLD PATH

www.JoePlum.com

www.ingramcontent.com/pod-product-compliance
Lightning Source LLC
Chambersburg PA
CBHW051659090426
42736CB00013B/2449